50 Mastering the BBQ Grill Recipes

By: Kelly Johnson

Table of Contents

- Classic BBQ Ribs
- Grilled Chicken Thighs with Lemon and Herb Marinade
- Pulled Pork Sandwiches
- Grilled Salmon with Garlic Butter
- BBQ Brisket
- Grilled Shrimp Skewers with Cajun Seasoning
- Grilled Vegetable Skewers
- Smoked Chicken Wings
- BBQ Beef Burgers
- Grilled Lamb Chops with Mint Yogurt Sauce
- Grilled Corn on the Cob with Chili Lime Butter
- BBQ Pork Belly
- Grilled Portobello Mushrooms with Balsamic Glaze
- BBQ Chicken Drumsticks
- Grilled Tofu Steaks with Teriyaki Sauce
- Grilled Sausages with Peppers and Onions
- Grilled Flatbread Pizza
- Grilled Pineapple with Brown Sugar and Cinnamon
- BBQ Pulled Chicken
- Grilled BBQ Meatballs
- Grilled Steak with Chimichurri Sauce
- BBQ Shrimp and Grits
- Grilled Fish Tacos with Mango Salsa
- BBQ Beef Short Ribs
- Grilled Eggplant with Tahini Dressing
- Grilled Stuffed Bell Peppers
- BBQ Beef Skewers
- Grilled Zucchini and Squash with Parmesan
- Grilled Clams with Garlic and Butter
- BBQ Pork Chops with Apple Slaw
- Grilled Sweet Potatoes with Honey Butter
- BBQ Chicken Skewers with Peanut Sauce
- Grilled Asparagus with Lemon and Parmesan
- Grilled Duck Breasts with Orange Glaze
- BBQ Turkey Legs

- Grilled Bacon-Wrapped Jalapeños
- Grilled Skirt Steak with Avocado Salsa
- Grilled Salmon Burgers with Dill Sauce
- BBQ Shrimp Po'Boy Sandwiches
- Grilled Avocados with Salsa Verde
- Grilled Rack of Lamb with Rosemary Garlic Marinade
- Grilled Chicken Caesar Salad
- BBQ Beer Can Chicken
- Grilled Vegetables with Pesto
- Grilled Sausage and Potato Packets
- BBQ Chicken Wings with Honey Mustard Glaze
- Grilled Octopus with Lemon and Olive Oil
- Grilled Shrimp and Chorizo Paella
- Grilled Flat Iron Steak with Roasted Garlic Butter
- BBQ Veggie Burgers

Classic BBQ Ribs

Ingredients:

- 2 racks of baby back ribs
- 1/4 cup olive oil
- Salt and pepper, to taste
- 1/4 cup brown sugar
- 2 tbsp paprika
- 1 tbsp garlic powder
- 1 tbsp onion powder
- 1 tsp cumin
- 1 tsp chili powder
- 1/2 tsp cayenne pepper
- 1 1/2 cups BBQ sauce

Instructions:

1. Preheat your grill or smoker to 225°F (107°C).
2. Remove the silver skin from the ribs and rub them with olive oil, salt, and pepper.
3. In a small bowl, mix together the brown sugar, paprika, garlic powder, onion powder, cumin, chili powder, and cayenne. Rub this spice mixture evenly over the ribs.
4. Place the ribs on the grill, bone-side down, and cook for 3-4 hours, maintaining a steady temperature. During the last 30 minutes, brush the ribs with BBQ sauce and continue grilling until they are tender and the sauce is caramelized.
5. Remove from the grill and let rest for 5-10 minutes before slicing and serving.

Grilled Chicken Thighs with Lemon and Herb Marinade

Ingredients:

- 8 bone-in, skin-on chicken thighs
- 2 tbsp olive oil
- Juice of 1 lemon
- 2 cloves garlic, minced
- 1 tbsp fresh thyme, chopped
- 1 tbsp fresh rosemary, chopped
- Salt and pepper to taste

Instructions:

1. In a bowl, combine the olive oil, lemon juice, garlic, thyme, rosemary, salt, and pepper.
2. Place the chicken thighs in a resealable plastic bag or shallow dish and pour the marinade over them. Seal and refrigerate for at least 1 hour, preferably overnight.
3. Preheat the grill to medium-high heat. Remove the chicken from the marinade and place it on the grill, skin-side down.
4. Grill for 6-7 minutes per side, or until the internal temperature reaches 165°F (74°C). Let rest for a few minutes before serving.

Pulled Pork Sandwiches

Ingredients:

- 4 lb pork shoulder (bone-in or boneless)
- 2 tbsp olive oil
- Salt and pepper, to taste
- 1/2 cup apple cider vinegar
- 1/2 cup BBQ sauce
- 1/2 cup chicken broth
- 1 onion, sliced
- 8 sandwich buns

Instructions:

1. Preheat the grill or slow cooker to low heat.
2. Rub the pork shoulder with olive oil, salt, and pepper. Place it on the grill (or in the slow cooker) and cook for 6-8 hours until tender.
3. In a separate bowl, combine the apple cider vinegar, BBQ sauce, and chicken broth.
4. Once the pork is cooked, remove it from the heat and shred it with two forks. Pour the sauce mixture over the pulled pork and toss to coat.
5. Serve the pulled pork on sandwich buns with extra BBQ sauce if desired.

Grilled Salmon with Garlic Butter

Ingredients:

- 4 salmon fillets, skin on
- 2 tbsp olive oil
- Salt and pepper, to taste
- 1/4 cup unsalted butter, melted
- 2 cloves garlic, minced
- 1 tbsp fresh lemon juice
- Fresh parsley, chopped

Instructions:

1. Preheat your grill to medium-high heat.
2. Brush the salmon fillets with olive oil and season with salt and pepper.
3. In a small bowl, mix the melted butter with garlic and lemon juice.
4. Place the salmon fillets on the grill, skin-side down, and cook for 4-5 minutes per side, or until the salmon is cooked through and flakes easily with a fork.
5. Brush the garlic butter over the salmon fillets and sprinkle with fresh parsley before serving.

BBQ Brisket

Ingredients:

- 5 lb beef brisket
- 1/4 cup olive oil
- Salt and pepper, to taste
- 2 tbsp paprika
- 1 tbsp brown sugar
- 1 tbsp garlic powder
- 1 tbsp onion powder
- 1 tsp cumin
- 2 cups BBQ sauce

Instructions:

1. Preheat your grill or smoker to 225°F (107°C).
2. Rub the brisket with olive oil, salt, and pepper. Then coat with paprika, brown sugar, garlic powder, onion powder, and cumin.
3. Place the brisket on the grill or smoker, fat-side up, and cook for 8-10 hours until tender. Maintain a consistent temperature.
4. Brush with BBQ sauce during the last 30 minutes of cooking.
5. Let the brisket rest for 15 minutes before slicing and serving.

Grilled Shrimp Skewers with Cajun Seasoning

Ingredients:

- 1 lb large shrimp, peeled and deveined
- 2 tbsp olive oil
- 2 tbsp Cajun seasoning
- 1 tbsp lemon juice
- 2 cloves garlic, minced
- Wooden skewers (soaked in water for 30 minutes)

Instructions:

1. In a bowl, toss the shrimp with olive oil, Cajun seasoning, lemon juice, and garlic.
2. Thread the shrimp onto the soaked skewers.
3. Preheat the grill to medium-high heat.
4. Grill the shrimp for 2-3 minutes per side, until they turn pink and are cooked through.
5. Serve with extra lemon wedges and garnish with fresh herbs if desired.

Grilled Vegetable Skewers

Ingredients:

- 1 zucchini, sliced
- 1 bell pepper, cut into chunks
- 1 red onion, cut into chunks
- 1 cup cherry tomatoes
- 1/2 cup olive oil
- 2 tbsp balsamic vinegar
- 1 tsp dried oregano
- Salt and pepper, to taste
- Wooden skewers (soaked in water for 30 minutes)

Instructions:

1. In a bowl, combine the olive oil, balsamic vinegar, oregano, salt, and pepper.
2. Thread the vegetables onto the soaked skewers.
3. Preheat the grill to medium heat.
4. Grill the vegetable skewers for 4-5 minutes per side until tender and lightly charred.
5. Serve immediately as a side dish or over rice.

Smoked Chicken Wings

Ingredients:

- 12 chicken wings, split and tips removed
- 2 tbsp olive oil
- 1 tbsp paprika
- 1 tbsp garlic powder
- 1 tbsp onion powder
- 1 tsp cayenne pepper
- Salt and pepper to taste
- 1/4 cup BBQ sauce

Instructions:

1. Preheat your smoker to 225°F (107°C).
2. Rub the chicken wings with olive oil and season with paprika, garlic powder, onion powder, cayenne, salt, and pepper.
3. Place the wings on the smoker and cook for 1.5-2 hours, flipping halfway through, until they are cooked through and crispy.
4. During the last 10 minutes, brush the wings with BBQ sauce and smoke until the sauce has set.
5. Serve with extra sauce on the side.

BBQ Beef Burgers

Ingredients:

- 1 lb ground beef (80% lean)
- Salt and pepper, to taste
- 4 burger buns
- 4 slices cheddar cheese (optional)
- Lettuce, tomato, pickles, and your favorite condiments

Instructions:

1. Preheat your grill to medium-high heat.
2. Form the ground beef into 4 equal-sized patties. Season both sides with salt and pepper.
3. Place the patties on the grill and cook for 4-5 minutes per side, or until they reach your desired doneness.
4. If using cheese, place a slice on each burger during the last minute of cooking and close the grill lid to melt the cheese.
5. Toast the buns on the grill for 1-2 minutes until golden.
6. Assemble the burgers by placing each patty on a bun and topping with lettuce, tomato, pickles, and condiments. Serve immediately.

Grilled Lamb Chops with Mint Yogurt Sauce

Ingredients:

- 8 lamb chops
- 2 tbsp olive oil
- 1 tbsp fresh rosemary, chopped
- 2 cloves garlic, minced
- Salt and pepper, to taste
- 1/2 cup Greek yogurt
- 2 tbsp fresh mint, chopped
- 1 tbsp lemon juice
- 1 tsp honey

Instructions:

1. Preheat your grill to medium-high heat.
2. Rub the lamb chops with olive oil, rosemary, garlic, salt, and pepper.
3. Grill the lamb chops for 4-5 minutes per side, or until they reach your desired level of doneness.
4. In a small bowl, combine the Greek yogurt, mint, lemon juice, and honey. Mix well.
5. Serve the grilled lamb chops with a dollop of the mint yogurt sauce on top.

Grilled Corn on the Cob with Chili Lime Butter

Ingredients:

- 4 ears of corn, husked
- 1/4 cup unsalted butter, softened
- 1 tbsp chili powder
- 1 tsp lime zest
- 1 tbsp lime juice
- Salt, to taste

Instructions:

1. Preheat your grill to medium heat.
2. Brush the corn with a little oil to prevent sticking, then place it on the grill.
3. Grill the corn for 10-12 minutes, turning occasionally, until it is tender and slightly charred.
4. In a small bowl, mix together the softened butter, chili powder, lime zest, lime juice, and salt.
5. Once the corn is cooked, brush it generously with the chili lime butter. Serve immediately.

BBQ Pork Belly

Ingredients:

- 2 lbs pork belly, skin-on
- 2 tbsp olive oil
- 1 tbsp smoked paprika
- 1 tsp garlic powder
- 1 tbsp brown sugar
- Salt and pepper, to taste
- 1/4 cup BBQ sauce

Instructions:

1. Preheat your grill to medium heat.
2. Rub the pork belly with olive oil, paprika, garlic powder, brown sugar, salt, and pepper.
3. Place the pork belly on the grill, skin-side down, and cook for 15-20 minutes, flipping occasionally, until the skin is crispy and the meat is tender.
4. Brush with BBQ sauce during the last 5 minutes of cooking.
5. Slice into bite-sized pieces and serve with extra BBQ sauce.

Grilled Portobello Mushrooms with Balsamic Glaze

Ingredients:

- 4 large Portobello mushrooms, stems removed
- 2 tbsp olive oil
- 2 tbsp balsamic vinegar
- 1 tbsp honey
- Salt and pepper, to taste

Instructions:

1. Preheat your grill to medium heat.
2. Brush the mushroom caps with olive oil and season with salt and pepper.
3. Grill the mushrooms, gill-side down, for 5-7 minutes per side, until they are tender.
4. In a small saucepan, combine the balsamic vinegar and honey. Simmer over medium heat for 5 minutes, or until the mixture thickens into a glaze.
5. Drizzle the balsamic glaze over the grilled mushrooms before serving.

BBQ Chicken Drumsticks

Ingredients:

- 8 chicken drumsticks
- 2 tbsp olive oil
- 1 tbsp paprika
- 1 tbsp garlic powder
- 1 tsp onion powder
- Salt and pepper, to taste
- 1/2 cup BBQ sauce

Instructions:

1. Preheat your grill to medium heat.
2. Rub the drumsticks with olive oil, paprika, garlic powder, onion powder, salt, and pepper.
3. Grill the drumsticks for 25-30 minutes, turning occasionally, until they reach an internal temperature of 165°F (74°C).
4. Brush with BBQ sauce during the last 5 minutes of grilling.
5. Serve with extra sauce on the side.

Grilled Tofu Steaks with Teriyaki Sauce

Ingredients:

- 1 block firm tofu, pressed and sliced into 1-inch steaks
- 2 tbsp olive oil
- Salt and pepper, to taste
- 1/4 cup teriyaki sauce
- 1 tbsp sesame seeds (optional)
- 2 green onions, chopped (optional)

Instructions:

1. Preheat your grill to medium heat.
2. Brush the tofu steaks with olive oil and season with salt and pepper.
3. Grill the tofu steaks for 4-5 minutes per side, until they are lightly charred and heated through.
4. Brush with teriyaki sauce during the last 2 minutes of grilling.
5. Garnish with sesame seeds and green onions before serving.

Grilled Sausages with Peppers and Onions

Ingredients:

- 4 sausages (your choice of flavor)
- 2 bell peppers, sliced
- 1 large onion, sliced
- 2 tbsp olive oil
- Salt and pepper, to taste
- 4 hoagie rolls (optional)

Instructions:

1. Preheat your grill to medium heat.
2. Grill the sausages for 8-10 minutes, turning occasionally, until fully cooked and browned.
3. Meanwhile, toss the bell peppers and onions with olive oil, salt, and pepper. Grill the vegetables for 4-5 minutes, until tender and slightly charred.
4. Serve the sausages in hoagie rolls, topped with grilled peppers and onions.

Grilled Flatbread Pizza

Ingredients:

- 2 flatbreads or naan breads
- 1/2 cup tomato sauce or pesto
- 1 cup shredded mozzarella cheese
- 1/2 cup sliced pepperoni or vegetables (like mushrooms, bell peppers, and onions)
- Olive oil, for brushing
- Fresh basil leaves, for garnish

Instructions:

1. Preheat your grill to medium-high heat.
2. Brush both sides of the flatbreads with olive oil.
3. Place the flatbreads on the grill, cooking for 2-3 minutes per side until they are lightly browned and crispy.
4. Remove from the grill and spread a thin layer of tomato sauce or pesto on top.
5. Top with mozzarella cheese and your desired toppings.
6. Return to the grill for 3-5 minutes until the cheese is melted and bubbly.
7. Remove from the grill, garnish with fresh basil leaves, slice, and serve.

Grilled Pineapple with Brown Sugar and Cinnamon

Ingredients:

- 1 fresh pineapple, peeled, cored, and cut into rings
- 2 tbsp brown sugar
- 1 tsp ground cinnamon
- 1 tbsp honey (optional)

Instructions:

1. Preheat your grill to medium heat.
2. In a small bowl, mix together the brown sugar and cinnamon.
3. Brush the pineapple rings with a little honey, then sprinkle the sugar-cinnamon mixture over the top.
4. Place the pineapple rings on the grill and cook for 2-3 minutes per side, until caramelized and grill marks appear.
5. Serve warm as a sweet side or dessert.

BBQ Pulled Chicken

Ingredients:

- 4 boneless, skinless chicken breasts
- 1 cup BBQ sauce
- 1/2 cup chicken broth
- 1 tbsp olive oil
- Salt and pepper, to taste
- 4 hamburger buns

Instructions:

1. Preheat your grill to medium heat.
2. Season the chicken breasts with salt and pepper and drizzle with olive oil.
3. Grill the chicken for 6-7 minutes per side, or until fully cooked and the internal temperature reaches 165°F (74°C).
4. Remove from the grill and let the chicken rest for 5 minutes.
5. Shred the chicken using two forks, then mix with BBQ sauce and chicken broth.
6. Serve the pulled chicken on hamburger buns with additional BBQ sauce if desired.

Grilled BBQ Meatballs

Ingredients:

- 1 lb ground beef or turkey
- 1/2 cup breadcrumbs
- 1 egg
- 1/4 cup grated Parmesan cheese
- 1 tbsp fresh parsley, chopped
- 1/2 tsp garlic powder
- Salt and pepper, to taste
- 1 cup BBQ sauce

Instructions:

1. Preheat your grill to medium heat.
2. In a bowl, combine the ground meat, breadcrumbs, egg, Parmesan, parsley, garlic powder, salt, and pepper.
3. Shape the mixture into 1-inch meatballs.
4. Thread the meatballs onto skewers or place them directly on the grill.
5. Grill for 8-10 minutes, turning occasionally, until the meatballs are cooked through.
6. Brush the meatballs with BBQ sauce during the last few minutes of grilling.
7. Serve the grilled meatballs with extra BBQ sauce for dipping.

Grilled Steak with Chimichurri Sauce

Ingredients:

- 2 ribeye or flank steaks (or your preferred cut)
- Salt and pepper, to taste
- 1/4 cup olive oil
- 2 tbsp red wine vinegar
- 2 garlic cloves, minced
- 1 cup fresh parsley, chopped
- 1 tbsp fresh oregano, chopped
- 1/2 tsp red pepper flakes

Instructions:

1. Preheat your grill to high heat.
2. Season the steaks with salt and pepper.
3. Grill the steaks for 4-6 minutes per side, or until your desired doneness is achieved.
4. In a bowl, whisk together the olive oil, red wine vinegar, garlic, parsley, oregano, and red pepper flakes to make the chimichurri sauce.
5. Serve the grilled steaks with the chimichurri sauce drizzled on top.

BBQ Shrimp and Grits

Ingredients:

- 1 lb shrimp, peeled and deveined
- 2 tbsp olive oil
- 1 tbsp smoked paprika
- 1 tsp garlic powder
- Salt and pepper, to taste
- 1 cup stone-ground grits
- 4 cups water or chicken broth
- 1/4 cup heavy cream
- 1 tbsp butter
- 1/4 cup grated cheddar cheese (optional)

Instructions:

1. Preheat your grill to medium-high heat.
2. Toss the shrimp with olive oil, paprika, garlic powder, salt, and pepper.
3. Grill the shrimp for 2-3 minutes per side, or until pink and cooked through.
4. Meanwhile, bring the water or chicken broth to a boil in a saucepan, then add the grits. Lower the heat and simmer, stirring occasionally, until thickened (about 20 minutes).
5. Stir in the cream, butter, and cheese into the grits.
6. Serve the shrimp over the creamy grits, garnished with fresh herbs if desired.

Grilled Fish Tacos with Mango Salsa

Ingredients:

- 4 white fish fillets (like tilapia or cod)
- 1 tbsp olive oil
- 1 tsp chili powder
- 1/2 tsp cumin
- Salt and pepper, to taste
- 8 small tortillas
- 1 mango, peeled and diced
- 1/2 red onion, diced
- 1/4 cup cilantro, chopped
- 1 tbsp lime juice
- 1/4 cup sour cream

Instructions:

1. Preheat your grill to medium heat.
2. Brush the fish fillets with olive oil and season with chili powder, cumin, salt, and pepper.
3. Grill the fish for 3-4 minutes per side, or until it flakes easily with a fork.
4. Meanwhile, combine the diced mango, onion, cilantro, and lime juice to make the salsa.
5. Warm the tortillas on the grill for 1-2 minutes.
6. Assemble the tacos by placing the grilled fish in the tortillas, topping with mango salsa and a drizzle of sour cream.

BBQ Beef Short Ribs

Ingredients:

- 4 beef short ribs
- 2 tbsp olive oil
- 2 tbsp BBQ rub (store-bought or homemade)
- 1 cup BBQ sauce

Instructions:

1. Preheat your grill to medium heat.
2. Rub the beef short ribs with olive oil and BBQ rub.
3. Grill the ribs for 2-3 hours, turning occasionally, until they are tender and cooked through. Optionally, you can cook the ribs over indirect heat for a longer period for extra tenderness.
4. During the last 20 minutes of grilling, brush the ribs with BBQ sauce.
5. Serve the tender, smoky short ribs with additional BBQ sauce on the side.

Grilled Eggplant with Tahini Dressing

Ingredients:

- 2 medium eggplants, sliced into 1/2-inch thick rounds
- 3 tbsp olive oil
- Salt and pepper, to taste
- 1/2 cup tahini
- 2 tbsp lemon juice
- 1 garlic clove, minced
- 1 tbsp water (to thin the dressing)
- Fresh parsley, chopped (for garnish)

Instructions:

1. Preheat your grill to medium-high heat.
2. Brush the eggplant slices with olive oil and season with salt and pepper.
3. Grill the eggplant slices for 3-4 minutes per side until they are tender and have grill marks.
4. In a bowl, whisk together tahini, lemon juice, garlic, and water until smooth.
5. Drizzle the tahini dressing over the grilled eggplant and garnish with fresh parsley. Serve warm.

Grilled Stuffed Bell Peppers

Ingredients:

- 4 large bell peppers, tops cut off and seeds removed
- 1 cup cooked quinoa or rice
- 1 cup black beans, drained and rinsed
- 1/2 cup shredded cheese (cheddar, mozzarella, or your choice)
- 1/2 cup diced tomatoes
- 1 tsp cumin
- 1/2 tsp chili powder
- Salt and pepper, to taste
- 1 tbsp olive oil

Instructions:

1. Preheat the grill to medium heat.
2. In a mixing bowl, combine the cooked quinoa or rice, black beans, cheese, diced tomatoes, cumin, chili powder, salt, and pepper.
3. Stuff each bell pepper with the mixture and drizzle with olive oil.
4. Wrap the peppers in foil and place them on the grill.
5. Grill for 25-30 minutes, or until the peppers are tender and the filling is heated through.
6. Serve warm, optionally garnished with fresh cilantro.

BBQ Beef Skewers

Ingredients:

- 1 lb beef sirloin or tenderloin, cut into 1-inch cubes
- 1/4 cup olive oil
- 2 tbsp soy sauce
- 2 tbsp BBQ sauce
- 1 tbsp Worcestershire sauce
- 1 tbsp honey
- 2 garlic cloves, minced
- Salt and pepper, to taste
- 1 red bell pepper, cut into chunks
- 1 onion, cut into chunks
- 1 zucchini, sliced

Instructions:

1. Preheat the grill to medium-high heat.
2. In a bowl, combine olive oil, soy sauce, BBQ sauce, Worcestershire sauce, honey, garlic, salt, and pepper to make the marinade.
3. Add the beef cubes to the marinade and let it sit for at least 30 minutes (or overnight).
4. Thread the beef, bell pepper, onion, and zucchini onto skewers.
5. Grill the skewers for 8-10 minutes, turning occasionally, until the beef reaches your desired doneness.
6. Serve the skewers with extra BBQ sauce on the side.

Grilled Zucchini and Squash with Parmesan

Ingredients:

- 2 zucchini, sliced into 1/2-inch thick rounds
- 2 yellow squash, sliced into 1/2-inch thick rounds
- 2 tbsp olive oil
- Salt and pepper, to taste
- 1/4 cup grated Parmesan cheese
- Fresh basil leaves, chopped (for garnish)

Instructions:

1. Preheat your grill to medium heat.
2. Drizzle the zucchini and squash slices with olive oil and season with salt and pepper.
3. Grill the vegetables for 2-3 minutes per side until they are tender and have grill marks.
4. Remove from the grill and sprinkle with grated Parmesan cheese while still hot.
5. Garnish with fresh basil and serve immediately.

Grilled Clams with Garlic and Butter

Ingredients:

- 2 dozen fresh clams, scrubbed clean
- 4 tbsp butter, melted
- 2 garlic cloves, minced
- 1 tbsp fresh parsley, chopped
- 1 tbsp lemon juice
- Salt and pepper, to taste

Instructions:

1. Preheat your grill to medium heat.
2. Place the clams on the grill grates and close the lid. Grill for 5-7 minutes until the shells open.
3. While the clams are grilling, mix melted butter, garlic, parsley, lemon juice, salt, and pepper in a small bowl.
4. Once the clams are open, remove them from the grill and drizzle with the garlic butter mixture.
5. Serve the grilled clams with a sprinkle of fresh parsley and extra lemon wedges.

BBQ Pork Chops with Apple Slaw

Ingredients:

- 4 bone-in pork chops
- 1/4 cup BBQ sauce
- Salt and pepper, to taste
- 1/2 head green cabbage, shredded
- 1 apple, julienned
- 1/4 cup mayonnaise
- 1 tbsp apple cider vinegar
- 1 tsp honey
- Salt and pepper, to taste

Instructions:

1. Preheat your grill to medium-high heat.
2. Season the pork chops with salt, pepper, and brush with BBQ sauce.
3. Grill the pork chops for 5-7 minutes per side, or until the internal temperature reaches 145°F (63°C).
4. While the pork chops are grilling, make the apple slaw by combining cabbage, apple, mayonnaise, apple cider vinegar, honey, salt, and pepper in a bowl.
5. Serve the grilled pork chops with a side of apple slaw.

Grilled Sweet Potatoes with Honey Butter

Ingredients:

- 4 medium sweet potatoes, peeled and cut into 1/2-inch thick rounds
- 2 tbsp olive oil
- Salt and pepper, to taste
- 2 tbsp butter, melted
- 1 tbsp honey
- Fresh thyme, for garnish

Instructions:

1. Preheat your grill to medium heat.
2. Drizzle the sweet potato rounds with olive oil and season with salt and pepper.
3. Grill the sweet potatoes for 4-5 minutes per side, until tender and grill marks appear.
4. In a small bowl, mix the melted butter and honey.
5. Drizzle the honey butter over the grilled sweet potatoes and garnish with fresh thyme. Serve warm.

BBQ Chicken Skewers with Peanut Sauce

Ingredients:

- 1 lb chicken breast, cut into 1-inch cubes
- 2 tbsp olive oil
- 2 tbsp soy sauce
- 1 tbsp lime juice
- 1 tbsp honey
- Salt and pepper, to taste
- 1/2 cup peanut butter
- 1 tbsp soy sauce
- 1 tbsp lime juice
- 1 tbsp honey
- 2 tbsp warm water (to thin the sauce)

Instructions:

1. Preheat your grill to medium-high heat.
2. In a bowl, combine olive oil, soy sauce, lime juice, honey, salt, and pepper. Marinate the chicken cubes in the mixture for at least 30 minutes.
3. Thread the marinated chicken onto skewers.
4. Grill the skewers for 5-7 minutes per side, or until the chicken is fully cooked (internal temperature of 165°F / 74°C).
5. While the chicken is grilling, make the peanut sauce by whisking together peanut butter, soy sauce, lime juice, honey, and warm water in a bowl until smooth.
6. Serve the grilled chicken skewers with the peanut sauce on the side.

Grilled Asparagus with Lemon and Parmesan

Ingredients:

- 1 lb fresh asparagus, trimmed
- 2 tbsp olive oil
- Salt and pepper, to taste
- Zest of 1 lemon
- 1/4 cup grated Parmesan cheese
- Fresh lemon wedges, for serving

Instructions:

1. Preheat your grill to medium heat.
2. Drizzle the asparagus with olive oil and season with salt and pepper.
3. Grill the asparagus for 4-6 minutes, turning occasionally, until tender and lightly charred.
4. Remove from the grill and sprinkle with lemon zest and grated Parmesan.
5. Serve with fresh lemon wedges.

Grilled Duck Breasts with Orange Glaze

Ingredients:

- 2 duck breasts, skin-on
- Salt and pepper, to taste
- 1/2 cup fresh orange juice
- 2 tbsp honey
- 1 tbsp soy sauce
- 1 tsp cornstarch (optional, for thickening)

Instructions:

1. Preheat your grill to medium-high heat.
2. Score the skin of the duck breasts in a crisscross pattern, being careful not to cut into the meat. Season with salt and pepper.
3. Place the duck breasts on the grill, skin-side down. Grill for 6-8 minutes, until the skin is crispy. Flip the breasts and grill for an additional 4-5 minutes for medium-rare.
4. While the duck is grilling, prepare the orange glaze by combining orange juice, honey, soy sauce, and cornstarch (if using) in a small saucepan over medium heat. Simmer for 5-7 minutes until the sauce thickens.
5. Drizzle the orange glaze over the grilled duck breasts before serving.

BBQ Turkey Legs

Ingredients:

- 4 turkey legs
- 1/4 cup olive oil
- Salt and pepper, to taste
- 1 tbsp smoked paprika
- 1 tbsp garlic powder
- 1 tbsp onion powder
- 1/2 cup BBQ sauce (optional)

Instructions:

1. Preheat your grill to medium heat.
2. Rub the turkey legs with olive oil, salt, pepper, smoked paprika, garlic powder, and onion powder.
3. Grill the turkey legs for 45-60 minutes, turning occasionally, until the internal temperature reaches 165°F (74°C).
4. In the last 10 minutes of grilling, brush the turkey legs with BBQ sauce, if desired.
5. Remove from the grill and let rest for 5 minutes before serving.

Grilled Bacon-Wrapped Jalapeños

Ingredients:

- 8 large jalapeños, halved and seeds removed
- 8 oz cream cheese, softened
- 1/2 cup shredded cheddar cheese
- 8 strips of bacon
- Toothpicks

Instructions:

1. Preheat your grill to medium heat.
2. Mix the cream cheese and shredded cheddar in a bowl.
3. Stuff the jalapeño halves with the cream cheese mixture.
4. Wrap each stuffed jalapeño with a strip of bacon and secure with a toothpick.
5. Grill the bacon-wrapped jalapeños for 6-8 minutes, turning occasionally, until the bacon is crispy and the jalapeños are tender.
6. Serve warm.

Grilled Skirt Steak with Avocado Salsa

Ingredients:

- 1 lb skirt steak
- 2 tbsp olive oil
- Salt and pepper, to taste
- 1 avocado, diced
- 1 small red onion, diced
- 1/2 cup cherry tomatoes, halved
- 1 tbsp fresh cilantro, chopped
- 1 tbsp lime juice

Instructions:

1. Preheat your grill to high heat.
2. Rub the skirt steak with olive oil and season with salt and pepper.
3. Grill the steak for 3-4 minutes per side for medium-rare, or longer for your desired doneness.
4. While the steak is grilling, make the avocado salsa by combining avocado, red onion, cherry tomatoes, cilantro, and lime juice in a bowl. Season with salt and pepper.
5. Let the steak rest for 5 minutes before slicing against the grain.
6. Top the sliced steak with the avocado salsa and serve.

Grilled Salmon Burgers with Dill Sauce

Ingredients:

- 1 lb fresh salmon, skin removed and chopped into chunks
- 1/4 cup breadcrumbs
- 1 egg
- 1 tbsp Dijon mustard
- 1 tbsp lemon juice
- Salt and pepper, to taste
- 4 burger buns
- 1/2 cup sour cream
- 2 tbsp fresh dill, chopped
- 1 tbsp lemon juice

Instructions:

1. Preheat your grill to medium-high heat.
2. In a food processor, pulse the salmon, breadcrumbs, egg, Dijon mustard, lemon juice, salt, and pepper until it forms a thick paste. Shape the mixture into 4 patties.
3. Grill the salmon burgers for 3-4 minutes per side, or until cooked through.
4. While the burgers are grilling, mix sour cream, dill, and lemon juice in a bowl to make the dill sauce.
5. Toast the burger buns on the grill for 1-2 minutes.
6. Serve the salmon burgers on the toasted buns with a generous dollop of dill sauce.

BBQ Shrimp Po'Boy Sandwiches

Ingredients:

- 1 lb large shrimp, peeled and deveined
- 2 tbsp olive oil
- 1 tbsp Cajun seasoning
- 1/2 cup mayonnaise
- 1 tbsp hot sauce
- 1 tbsp lemon juice
- 4 soft hoagie rolls
- Shredded lettuce
- Sliced tomatoes

Instructions:

1. Preheat your grill to medium-high heat.
2. Toss the shrimp with olive oil and Cajun seasoning.
3. Grill the shrimp for 2-3 minutes per side until pink and cooked through.
4. While the shrimp are grilling, mix mayonnaise, hot sauce, and lemon juice in a small bowl.
5. Toast the hoagie rolls on the grill for 1-2 minutes.
6. Assemble the Po'Boy sandwiches by spreading the spicy mayo on the rolls, adding lettuce and tomato, and topping with the grilled shrimp.

Grilled Avocados with Salsa Verde

Ingredients:

- 4 ripe avocados, halved and pitted
- 1 tbsp olive oil
- Salt and pepper, to taste
- 1/2 cup salsa verde (store-bought or homemade)
- Fresh cilantro, for garnish

Instructions:

1. Preheat your grill to medium heat.
2. Brush the avocado halves with olive oil and season with salt and pepper.
3. Grill the avocados, flesh-side down, for 3-4 minutes until grill marks appear and they are slightly softened.
4. Remove from the grill and top with salsa verde.
5. Garnish with fresh cilantro and serve.

Grilled Rack of Lamb with Rosemary Garlic Marinade

Ingredients:

- 1 rack of lamb (8 ribs)
- 2 tbsp olive oil
- 4 garlic cloves, minced
- 2 tbsp fresh rosemary, chopped
- 1 tbsp fresh thyme, chopped
- Zest of 1 lemon
- Salt and pepper, to taste

Instructions:

1. Preheat your grill to medium-high heat.
2. In a small bowl, combine olive oil, garlic, rosemary, thyme, lemon zest, salt, and pepper.
3. Rub the lamb rack with the marinade, ensuring it's well-coated. Let it marinate for at least 30 minutes.
4. Grill the lamb rack, fat side down, for 4-5 minutes, then flip and cook for another 4-5 minutes. Continue grilling for 20-25 minutes, turning occasionally, until the internal temperature reaches 130°F (54°C) for medium-rare.
5. Let the lamb rest for 5 minutes before slicing between the ribs and serving.

Grilled Chicken Caesar Salad

Ingredients:

- 2 boneless skinless chicken breasts
- 1 tbsp olive oil
- Salt and pepper, to taste
- 4 cups romaine lettuce, chopped
- 1/4 cup grated Parmesan cheese
- 1/4 cup Caesar dressing
- Croutons (optional)

Instructions:

1. Preheat your grill to medium-high heat.
2. Brush the chicken breasts with olive oil and season with salt and pepper.
3. Grill the chicken for 6-7 minutes per side, until cooked through (internal temperature should be 165°F or 74°C).
4. While the chicken is grilling, toss the chopped lettuce with Caesar dressing and top with grated Parmesan cheese.
5. Once the chicken is cooked, slice it thinly and place it on top of the salad. Garnish with croutons, if desired. Serve immediately.

BBQ Beer Can Chicken

Ingredients:

- 1 whole chicken (about 4-5 lbs)
- 1 can of beer (preferably a lager or pale ale)
- 2 tbsp olive oil
- 1 tbsp paprika
- 1 tsp garlic powder
- 1 tsp onion powder
- 1 tsp salt
- 1/2 tsp black pepper
- 1/2 tsp cayenne pepper (optional)

Instructions:

1. Preheat your grill to medium heat (about 375°F or 190°C).
2. Pat the chicken dry with paper towels and rub it with olive oil.
3. In a small bowl, mix together paprika, garlic powder, onion powder, salt, pepper, and cayenne pepper. Rub this spice mixture all over the chicken.
4. Open the beer can and take a few sips (or pour out a little). Insert the can into the cavity of the chicken, standing it upright on the grill.
5. Grill the chicken for 1 to 1.5 hours, until the internal temperature reaches 165°F (74°C) and the skin is golden brown and crispy.
6. Carefully remove the chicken from the grill and let it rest for 10 minutes before carving.

Grilled Vegetables with Pesto

Ingredients:

- 1 zucchini, sliced into rounds
- 1 bell pepper, sliced
- 1 red onion, sliced
- 8 oz cherry tomatoes
- 2 tbsp olive oil
- Salt and pepper, to taste
- 1/4 cup pesto sauce (store-bought or homemade)

Instructions:

1. Preheat your grill to medium heat.
2. Toss the vegetables with olive oil, salt, and pepper.
3. Grill the zucchini, bell pepper, onion, and tomatoes for about 4-6 minutes, turning occasionally, until tender and lightly charred.
4. Remove the vegetables from the grill and toss them with the pesto sauce.
5. Serve immediately as a side dish or over a bed of grains.

Grilled Sausage and Potato Packets

Ingredients:

- 4 sausages (Italian, bratwurst, or your choice)
- 4 medium potatoes, thinly sliced
- 1 red bell pepper, sliced
- 1 yellow onion, sliced
- 2 tbsp olive oil
- Salt and pepper, to taste
- 1 tsp smoked paprika
- Fresh parsley, for garnish (optional)

Instructions:

1. Preheat your grill to medium-high heat.
2. Slice the sausages into 2-3 inch pieces. In a large bowl, toss the sausage pieces, sliced potatoes, bell pepper, and onion with olive oil, salt, pepper, and smoked paprika.
3. Create individual foil packets by placing the sausage and vegetable mixture on large pieces of aluminum foil. Fold the edges to seal the packets.
4. Place the foil packets on the grill and cook for 20-25 minutes, turning occasionally, until the potatoes are tender and the sausages are cooked through.
5. Carefully open the packets (watch for steam!) and serve the sausage and potatoes with fresh parsley, if desired.

BBQ Chicken Wings with Honey Mustard Glaze

Ingredients:

- 12 chicken wings
- 1/4 cup honey
- 1/4 cup Dijon mustard
- 1 tbsp olive oil
- 1 tbsp apple cider vinegar
- 1 tsp garlic powder
- Salt and pepper, to taste

Instructions:

1. Preheat your grill to medium-high heat.
2. In a small bowl, whisk together honey, Dijon mustard, olive oil, apple cider vinegar, garlic powder, salt, and pepper to make the glaze.
3. Season the chicken wings with salt and pepper, then place them on the grill. Grill for about 20-25 minutes, turning occasionally, until the wings are crispy and cooked through (internal temperature of 165°F or 74°C).
4. Brush the wings with the honey mustard glaze during the last 5 minutes of grilling, allowing the glaze to caramelize.
5. Remove the wings from the grill and serve immediately with extra glaze for dipping.

Grilled Octopus with Lemon and Olive Oil

Ingredients:

- 2 octopus tentacles (about 1 lb)
- 2 tbsp olive oil
- 1 lemon, juiced
- 2 garlic cloves, minced
- Salt and pepper, to taste
- Fresh parsley, chopped (for garnish)

Instructions:

1. Preheat your grill to medium-high heat.
2. If the octopus is not tender, simmer it in a pot of water for 45-60 minutes until tender. Then, drain and let it cool slightly.
3. In a small bowl, combine olive oil, lemon juice, garlic, salt, and pepper.
4. Brush the octopus with the lemon and olive oil mixture.
5. Grill the octopus on medium-high heat for about 3-4 minutes per side, until it's charred and crispy on the outside.
6. Garnish with fresh parsley and serve with lemon wedges on the side.

Grilled Shrimp and Chorizo Paella

Ingredients:

- 1 lb shrimp, peeled and deveined
- 8 oz chorizo, sliced into rounds
- 1 cup Arborio rice
- 1/2 cup white wine
- 2 cups chicken broth
- 1/2 tsp smoked paprika
- 1/2 tsp saffron threads (optional)
- 1/2 cup frozen peas
- 1 red bell pepper, diced
- 2 tbsp olive oil
- Salt and pepper, to taste
- Fresh parsley, for garnish

Instructions:

1. Preheat your grill to medium heat. If using a grill-safe pan, place it on the grill.
2. Heat olive oil in a large, grill-safe skillet. Add the chorizo and cook for 5 minutes until browned, then remove from the skillet and set aside.
3. Add the shrimp to the skillet, season with salt, pepper, and smoked paprika, and cook for 2-3 minutes per side, until pink and cooked through. Remove and set aside.
4. In the same skillet, add the rice and toast it for 2 minutes. Pour in the white wine and cook until it evaporates.
5. Add chicken broth and saffron, if using. Bring to a simmer, then cover the skillet and let cook for 10-15 minutes, until the rice is cooked through and liquid is absorbed.
6. Stir in the peas, chorizo, and shrimp. Let everything heat through for another 2 minutes.
7. Garnish with fresh parsley and serve warm.

Grilled Flat Iron Steak with Roasted Garlic Butter

Ingredients:

- 2 flat iron steaks (about 6 oz each)
- 2 tbsp olive oil
- Salt and pepper, to taste
- 1/2 cup unsalted butter, softened
- 4 garlic cloves, minced
- 1 tbsp fresh parsley, chopped
- 1 tsp fresh thyme leaves

Instructions:

1. Preheat your grill to high heat.
2. Rub the steaks with olive oil and season generously with salt and pepper.
3. Grill the steaks for 4-5 minutes per side, or until the internal temperature reaches 130°F (54°C) for medium-rare, or adjust for your preferred doneness.
4. While the steaks are grilling, make the garlic butter: In a small bowl, combine softened butter, minced garlic, parsley, and thyme. Mix until smooth.
5. Remove the steaks from the grill and let rest for 5 minutes.
6. Top each steak with a dollop of the roasted garlic butter before serving.

BBQ Veggie Burgers

Ingredients:

- 1 can (15 oz) black beans, drained and mashed
- 1/2 cup breadcrumbs
- 1/4 cup grated carrot
- 1/4 cup corn kernels
- 1/4 cup finely chopped red onion
- 2 tbsp soy sauce
- 1 tbsp olive oil
- 1 tsp cumin
- Salt and pepper, to taste
- 4 whole wheat burger buns
- Optional toppings: lettuce, tomato, avocado, cheese, etc.

Instructions:

1. Preheat your grill to medium heat.
2. In a large bowl, combine mashed black beans, breadcrumbs, grated carrot, corn, onion, soy sauce, olive oil, cumin, salt, and pepper. Mix well to form a thick, firm mixture. If too wet, add more breadcrumbs.
3. Shape the mixture into 4 patties.
4. Grill the veggie burgers for 5-7 minutes per side, until golden brown and heated through.
5. Toast the burger buns on the grill for 1-2 minutes until lightly charred.
6. Assemble the burgers with your favorite toppings and serve immediately.

Printed in the USA
CPSIA information can be obtained
at www.ICGtesting.com
CBHW081522031224
18357CB00023B/95

9 798330 583775